Quick guide to starting a bullet journal

Take Back Control of Your Life and Your Day With These Great Bullet Journal Ideas

Levi Bailey

Why I Wrote This Book

What frustrated me most about traditional planners is that even though I had a calendar, and a to-do list, there were still so many things floating around in my life that I had no way to capture in one system. Ideas, notes, personal thoughts, future events, future action items, etc. all things that needed to be addressed. So what I ended up with was a planner, a separate notebook, a desk calendar, a pad of sticky notes, and a refrigerator whiteboard. All of which resulted in a disjointed system that kept me frustrated to no end. But when I discovered the concept of the bullet journal, it was as if a miracle had fallen upon me and I had seen the light. Literally. Now, with my bullet journal, I have one single system that I use to capture everything that matters most to me in my life. And the best part it is that I use it daily. My bullet journal stays with me all day. I refer to it all day. I update it everyday. and I love it as if it were the best thing that ever happened to me (next to my wife and kids of course). This book is a very quick and simple guide to get you up and running with a bullet journal as quickly as possible. Let's get started!

Table of Contents

Chapter 1. Introduction

The Problem With Traditional Planners

Many planners assume a one size fits all approach which is just plain silly in my opinion. Your planner is just as personal as you are (at least it should be). It represents you, your life, your day, your dreams, your hopes, your goals, and whatever else you use it for. The trouble with traditional planners is that they are so formulaic. They force you to conform to a blueprint that makes you to adapt to your planner, when it should be the other way around. Your planner should adapt to you. Sadly, that's just not the case. That is why we so often start the year with fresh planner in hand and a list of goals and action items ready to take on the world, only to abandon it before spring hits. And then the disorganization and chaos of your life continues on, leading to more frustration with each passing day.

I always wonder why all planners seem the same. Sure, they come in different sizes, with different covers, and important dates to remember and so on. But what about all the other stuff that matters to me? Did that not matter to the people who created them? Did they think my life should fit inside some little box that they defined for me? Evidently they did, because I have yet to find one that truly meets my needs. One that is unique to me. That's the thing with traditional planners. They aren't customizable, and they have no way to grow with you. Your needs change, your priorities change, your goals change, sometimes even daily. But most planners have no way to capture that change, at least not in any way that's not messy or disorganized. You know what I mean, the endless crossing out, erasing, hard to understand notes in the sidebar, and other crazy conventions we come up with to try to customize our planner to make it reflect the life we truly live. But all we end up with is a big messy book full of dates and scribble marks, that when reviewed at the end of the year, has very little meaning at all.

With a bullet journal, there is no way to screw up a system that you created. If you mess up something on a page, simply flip to the next page and correct course. Come up with something else that needs to be done? Simply add it to your future log (we'll talk more about this later in the book). The point is, the bullet journal grows with you, captures life's unexpected challenges, and allows you to manage your life and your day in a way that is organized, fluid, and adaptable to YOU!

And with a bullet journal, no matter how your brain works, the bullet journal keeps up. It is perfect for linear thinkers and abstract thinkers alike. No matter how your brain works, how you think, how you capture things, how you plan, a bullet journal is right there by your side to support you all the way.

Benefits of A Bullet Journal

Fosters greater engagement with planning and managing your life

The bullet journal system is a great way to foster greater engagement in planning and managing not just your day, but your life as well. Because it is a system that captures any and everything you can imagine in one place, you have a blank slate to create and play to your hearts content. And when you we create, play, and have fun with something, we become more engaged with it, more connected to it, and more likely to nurture it and help it to grow.

Free Pass

I am an incessant worrier. Have been my whole life. But my bullet journal has drastically reduced the amount of worry I carry around in my brain and in my gut everyday. When I worry about something, I simply write it down in my bullet journal. That way, I am free to get it out of my mind, knowing that I have it captured someplace that I can get back to when I am ready to address it. But you know what? It's not often that I need to get back to it. But my bullet journal is my "free pass" to forget about it for the moment, and get back to it later should I choose to. Or what about that action item that pops up that you can't address right away? Just write it in your bullet journal. Got a great idea that you don't want to loose? Your bullet journal is the best place for it. You can jot down all your ideas quickly and have an easy way to refer back to them when you are ready (we'll get to how in a bit).

How Important is It Really?

We all lead busy lives. And we all probably have a to-do list that spans the enter length of the Mississippi river. But do we ever get to them all? I sure don't. So why do I keep writing them down? Good question. I don't have the answer to that, but for me it's a bad habit that that my bullet journal has helped me to break. Because it is a manual system, it forces me to think about the importance of each action item before I write it down. Often, I find that well over half of the items that I thought were important, really are just time wasters and offer no value to my life. So now, what I have is a list of items that are truly important to me. Items that I know I am likely to address simply by the fact that it was important enough to me to write it down.

Re-engage In Your Life

I no longer wander around aimlessly throughout my day. My bullet journal stays with me all day, and I refer to it and update it all thorough the day. That is the beauty of this system, because with it, you have a place where you can manage everything in your life because you are actively engaging with your bullet journal throughout the day. And total immersion and engagement with your bullet journal is definitely a great way to totally engage in your life.

A Planner AND a Journal all in One

I have used the terms "planning" and "manage" a lot up until now, but it is important to note that a bullet journal is much more than that. It can also serve as your daily journal. A place to record your thoughts, your ideas, your reflections. Some people choose to use it simply as a planner. And some, like me, use it as a planner, a thought journal, a place to track new habits I am working on, and even a place to take notes on new things I am learning. It is definitely something that goes well beyond what one would normally consider a journal, or a planner.

It Truly Represents You

Personality is another key advantage to using a bullet journal. When you create something that is uniquely yours, it reflects, well, you! And it should. With a bullet journal, you can be assured that you have a system that is created uniquely for you, for your ideas, for your life, and for your plans. With a bullet journal, each page can be customized to your own liking. You can create your own calendar system, your own system for capturing action items, events, notes, and anything else you can think of.

So relaxing

When I say that your bullet journal is customization, I mean that literally. Your journal is also a wonderful way to express your creativity (whether you think you are creative or not). There are endless ways in which you can customize your journal. Many people get really elaborate with fancy lettering, colored pens, washi paper etc. If you take a look online, you'll get some great examples of the level of creativity that some people put into these. This is certainly not a required element of a bullet journal. You could stick to the basics. But I do recommend putting some level of creativity into your journal. I'm not talking Picasso quality work here (although if you've got it like that, go for it!). Just something outside the box of what you would normally do. Maybe fancy it up with some colored pens once and a while. I suggest this for several reasons. For one, it is a relaxing activity that will help to get your mind off of your day. If you are updating your journal at the end of the night, a little bit of art is a great way to unwind and give your brain a beak. It gives your brain something fun to focus on before going to sleep. And if you are updating your journal at the beginning of your day, it is a great way to wake up your brain and get you ready for your day. Like I said, this part isn't required at all. But your journal is supposed to be fun. It can be as fun as you make it.

Chapter 2. Setup - Gather Supplies

The Basics

There really isn't much that you need to start a bullet journal. Just a notebook and a pen or a pencil. That's it. There are some other tools you can use, which I'll talk about in a bit. But for just getting started, a notebook and a pen or pencil will do.

Notebook

My only suggestion here is in regards to the size of the notebook. Your bullet journal is meant to be something that you interact with throughout the day. Which means, you will carry it with you everyday. You don't want your journal to be so large that you won't take it with you. That just defeats the purpose. I would suggest an A5 size notebook or something small enough to to carry with you daily, but not so large that it becomes a forgotten item tucked away in the bottom of your desk drawer.

Pencil

A basic pen or pencil will do. However, I will offer a couple of suggestions here. And that would be a multicolored pen. You know, the kind where you click for blue, click for red, etc. I would also get the kind of multi-color pen that has a mechanical pencil incorporated. That way you'll have four colored pens and a pencil all in one pen

Advanced

There are so many ways in which your bullet journal can become your very own, with a personality to match yours. Let's take a look at a few tools that will help you take your bullet journal to the next level. These items aren't required. If you don't care about this, then you can just skip this section. But if you want some advice on tools that will help you get creative, then please continue reading.

Bullet Journal

The creator of the Bullet Journal system has a journal created specifically for this purpose. But you don't have to buy one of those. You can buy whatever style journal that you like (keeping in mind the suggestion about size mentioned earlier). I would also suggest buying a journal that has either grid lines or dotted pages. They make customizing things in your journal a lot easier as we'll see later.

Another one of my suggestions, is try to find one that has numbered pages and a few dedicated index pages. You'll need these to help you find information quickly in your journal.

Pens

Feel free to get whatever you like. I personally like the multicolored pens I talked about earlier. But because I am a writer, I am very fond of fountain pens and use them in my journal regularly. The fountain pens are great, but you have to make sure that you buy a journal that specifically states that you won't get any bleed through to the next page.

Markers

Markers and colored pencils are a great way to add a splash of color to your journal. Any good marker should work. The reason you may want to add color, is that it helps you to spot things on the page faster when you are scanning for information. Also, it's just fun.

Stickers

You can find stickers online pretty easily and at some of the big retail stores. Stickers can be used to point out or highlight important information. They add decor to your journal. And they make your journal something interesting, something you'll want to keep using.

Ruler

Your bullet journal won''t have anything in it to start but either grid lines or dots (depending on which style journal you bought). You will be drawing a lot of the things you need in it yourself. So a good ruler or straight edge is a great way to keep your lines straight and even.

Whatever Else You Want!

Chapter 3. Learn The Lingo

Before we get started, there is a bit of terminology that I want to cover. It will make the rest of the book a lot easier if we are on the same page about terminology.

The Original Lingo

The creator of the Bullet Journal system has a set of terminology that he created to keep track of information. We'll cover that first, then I'll give some ideas on some custom things I've created for myself. We'll also cover ways in which you can create your own symbols.

Symbols

Topics and Page Numbers

A topic is simply the topic of the information on the page in which you are writing. And the page number, is simply the number of the page you are writing on. I know this seems trivial, but it will all come together as we move on. For each page in your journal, you'll write a topic at the top of the page. Then you'll write the page number at the bottom of the page (you won't need to do your own page numbers if the journal you purchased is already numbered).

Tasks

Tasks are simply action items. Things that require you to do something. There are three types of tasks you'll work with in your journal. new tasks, completed tasks, and tasks that need further action.

-New Tasks are simply noted with a "bullet" to the left of it.

-Tasks that have been completed will get an "x" written over top of the bullet

-Tasks that you will do in the near future are noted with a right facing arrow symbol ">" after the dot

-Tasks that you will schedule for another time, that is not in the near future gets noted with a left facing arrow "<" after the dot

Bullets

Bullets are symbols used to denote items in your journal such as tasks, events, reminders, ideas, and notes. Each of these items will have a separate "bullet" associated with it, that represents at a glance what that item is.

Events

Events are denoted by the letter "o".

Notes

Notes are denoted with a dash "-" symbol

Signifiers

Signifiers are used to give extra meaning to your bullets.

-Priority - Represented by an asterisk or star "*" placed to the left of the bullet

-Inspiration - Represented by an exclamation point "!" to the left of the bullet

-Explore - Represented by an eye. These are things that require additional information or research

Modules

Future Log

The future log is simply the page where you'll plan your events and action items at a glance over a span of several months. Flip to a new page in your journal. Now with a ruler, block out 12 sections that span both pages. Now label each section with each month of the year. Then, transfer all of your known events to the proper month. Also add any action items that you'll need to address in each month. This is a great way to get a birds eye view of anything on your radar for the next several months. I personally like to use a 12 month spread, because I like to see the whole year at once. Be sure to write the page number at the bottom of the page, and create an index entry for this topic.

You'll use this future log regularly. Each day, as new events or future action items come up, you'll put them in your future log. And each day, as you are moving (often referred to as migrating) tasks to the next day, you may decide that you'll schedule things out a bit further in the future. Those items then get moved to your future log.

Monthly Log

The monthly log gives you a birds eye view of the current month. Here's how you create a monthly log. Simply open a new page in your journal. On the left hand page, in the far left column, write down the numbers of each day of the month going vertically down the page. Then next to each day, write the event or action item associated with that day.

On the right hand page, you can create a list of bullet action items that you want to complete during the month. These are items that don't necessarily need to get scheduled on any particular day. So, what you'll end up with is a spread for the current month that lists events, and all action items in one glance.

Daily Log

The daily log is really where you'll spend the most of your time. The daily log consists of appointments and action items for the day. As well as notes, ideas, or anything important that needs to be noted for the day. You could even do your diary/journal entry on your daily page. It's basically a way to capture and manage whatever is going on in your world for the day. In my bullet journal, I often put a positive quote at the top of the day. I also like to put at the top of my day, in very big lettering something sweet I plan to do for my wife that day, and something special that I plan to do for the kids that day. My daily log is where I like to get really creative with colored pens, stickers and sketch notes. It makes reviewing my week quite interesting.

Collections

Collections represent topic pages that contain just basic lists of common items. For example, a list of books you'd like to read. A list of places you'd like to visit. A grocery list for the month. The possibilities for collections are endless. Again, be sure you are creating page numbers, and index entries for each topic.

Index

The index is exactly what it sounds like. An index. Only it contains references to the topics that you've written in your journal. Each time you finish a page, go to your index and write the page number as well as the topic in your index. This way you'll have a way to quickly find the information for later reference. Many journals will have index pages in them, where all you need to do is write your topic and the page number in the allotted allotted space. If your journal did not come with this feature, it is easy to set up your own.

Go to the last page of your journal (or the beginning if it suits you). Draw some lines across both pages. These lines will hold an index entries. Don't worry about saving or allocating extra pages here. One page will do. Besides, if you run out of space in your current index, just create another one on your next available page, then reference it in your original index. This is another area where color coding can come in handy. You could write the important items in your index with a red marker, or any other color you choose. This will make it easy to identify those important items quickly when you need to.

Some of My Own Lingo

Symbols

Household Project or Chore

For my household projects or chores, I simply draw a little house

Family Time or Event

Family time, family events, or one of the kids practices gets denoted with a simple stick figure of a human. A bit crude, but it gets the point across.

Writing Activity

My writing time is captured as a triangle

Bright Idea

I usually draw a simple light bulb to represent any ideas that may pop into my head

Me Time or Fun Time

When I am planning or scheduling something fun or exciting for me, I'll use a happy face.

Marriage or Action Items For My Spouse

If it is an item related to my wife, for example something she has asked me to do, a date night, or what have you, I denote those with a heart. Needless to say, those items get priority when I am looking over my day.

Make Your Own

These are just some ideas to get your started. As I keep reiterating throughout this book, this journal is all yours. You can use the original symbols, but feel free to create your own symbols to things that have more meaning for you. After all, your journal doesn't need to sense to anyone but you.

Chapter 4. The Initial Setup

There's no real "right" way to setup your bullet journal or to get started. Here are a few things I recommend to get you going.

1. Setup your index page

2. Create a future log

3. Create a monthly log

4. Happy Bullet Journaling

Once you've got these items set up, I would sit down and do a complete brain dump. Gather up any old calendars or planners that are about to get dumped, sticky notes with action items, to do lists you've scribbled all over the place etc. Then take some time and get all these items logged in the appropriate place in your journal. Got something that doesn't seem to fit into any category we've discussed? Simply create your own. For example, I have tons of index cards with scenes that I've written for a current book or perhaps a new book I am writing. For these, I simply create a new page. Label it with the scene name or book name, and log it in my index. Then I toss the index card.

Chapter 5. The Bullet Journal In Action

How Exactly Do I Use It?

Sample Workflow of How I Use The Bullet Journal

Monthly Workflow

1. At the end of the current month is when I plan my upcoming month. I sit down, and migrate any items from last month over to the new month

2. I add any items that haven't been captured daily

3. I add some new goals for the month

The thing I'd like to point out, is that I don't do all of my monthly logs up front. There's really no need to as long as you are utilizing the future log. But the reason I don't, is because it gives me the flexibility to change the layout and look and feel of my monthly log every month. I may have found an idea for a monthly layout that I like better, and want to try it out. So, I don't want a bunch of wasted pages if I'm not going to use that layout for the month. But as always, do what suits you and have fun with it.

Weekly Workflow

1. Each week, I review items from the prior week that I need to migrate to the upcoming week.

2. I add any new items to the weekly log

3. I add any new items to the future log

4. I review my goals for the week and note progress, and make plans for what to accomplish the upcoming week

Daily Workflow

Mydaily workflow is pretty basic. I just open a new page in my journal, and migrate any tasks from the day before. Then I add any new tasks and reminders. I also review any appointments for the day and mark down any new upcoming appointments. I also use my daily page to record notes throughout the day, my daily gratitude list, positive quotes, doodles, and anything else that pops into my brain on any given day. Again, the point is to come up with your own workflow so that this system works for you and only you.

Migrating to a New Journal - What To Do When You Run Out of Pages

OK, so the inevitable has happened. You've run out of pages in your bullet journal. What do you do? If you guessed migration, you'd be correct. But migrating effectively and painlessly is something that requires a little bit of planning.

I suggest that you don't wait until you get to the very last page to migrate. Maybe start migrating a few pages before you run out. That way, you won't be stuck without a journal until you do migrate.

So the question is, what exactly do you migrate? Of course you can't migrate everything, nor should you. The choice is really yours, but here are some suggestions:

1. Monthly log for the current month

   2. Future log

3. Any collections that you'll refer to often. Some people will argue that this isn't necessary as long as you're indexing everything properly. That with the index, it shouldn't matter which journal your collections are in. I do agree with that to a certain point. I personally have collections that I refer to regularly, sometimes daily. I don't want to carry around a bunch of journals just to get to that information. So, the point here, is to migrate the collections that you'll definitely need to refer to often.

So that's it! A quick and easy guide to get you up and running with your very own bullet journal. The important thing to remember is to have fun, make it your own, and let it evolve with you. Happy planning!

About The Author

Levi Bailey is a writer and entrepreneur who is obsessed with all things "personal productivity". When not completely occupied with his bullet journal, he can be found spending quality time with his wife, two kids, and two "fur babies".

One Last Thing...

If you enjoyed this book or found it useful I'd be very grateful if you'd post a short review on Amazon. Your support really does make a difference and I read all the reviews personally so I can get your feedback and make this book even better.

Thanks again for your support!

Made in United States
North Haven, CT
30 December 2022